Biff and Chip went to stay with Gran.
Gran lived in a little village. Biff and Chip
liked staying with Gran. She was good fun.
She made Biff and Chip laugh.

Gran took Biff and Chip to the shed.
She had a surprise for them.

"Open the door," she said. "I've got a
surprise for you."

"What is it?" asked Chip.

Biff and Chip opened the door and
looked inside the shed. They had a big
surprise.

"Oh no!" said Biff. "There's a dragon in
the shed!"

"It's not a real dragon," said Gran. "It's
a kite."
Biff and Chip looked at the kite.
"It's a Chinese dragon kite," said Gran.
"It's wonderful," said Biff.

The children wanted to fly the kite.

"It's a good day for a picnic," said
Gran. "And it's a good day to fly the kite.
It's quite windy."

"Can I fly it first?" asked Biff.

Gran found a good place for the picnic. It was near her house.

"This is a good place to fly the kite," she said.

She let Biff fly the kite first.

The wind took the kite up in the sky. It went higher and higher.

"It looks wonderful," said Chip.

Suddenly the wind got stronger.

"Don't let go," called Gran.

The wind pulled the dragon kite out of
Biff's hand. It blew away and landed in a
tree. Biff was upset.

"I couldn't hold on to it," she said.

Chip climbed the tree and pulled the
kite, but it wouldn't come down.

"Be careful," said Biff. "Mind you don't
tear it."

"And mind you don't fall," said Gran.

The kite was stuck in the tree. Chip couldn't get it down. In the end, someone got the kite down with a long pole.

"Thank you," said Biff and Chip.

Biff and Chip went to fly the kite again.
Chip saw some wild flowers.

"Mind those flowers!" he said. "Don't
step on them."

Gran looked upset.

"What's the matter, Gran?" asked Chip.

"They want to build a motorway. They want to put it right here," said Gran.

Biff and Chip were upset, too. They
didn't want a motorway there.

"We won't be able to have picnics or
play in the wood," said Biff. "And we
won't be able to fly the kite."

A woman pointed to the wood. Then she
pointed to the village.

"This is where the motorway will go. It
will go between the wood and the village,"
she said.

Gran was very upset. She looked at the village and she looked at her house.

"We don't want a motorway here," she said. "We must stop it."

Gran told people in the village about the motorway. Everyone was upset.

"We don't want a motorway here. We must stop it," they said.

Everyone wanted to stop the motorway.

"We don't want it here," said Gran. "It will spoil our village."

"It can't be helped," said a man. "We can't stop it."

People came to Gran's house. They
made banners and posters. Gran made a
big banner. Biff helped her. The banner
said, "Stop the motorway".

Chip was good at painting. He made a
poster. The poster said, "Save our woodland".
"The banner looks good," said Biff. "And
Chip's poster looks good too."

Everyone went to a meeting. An
important woman was there. The woman
pointed to a map.

"We have to put the motorway here,"
she said.

"We don't want the motorway here,"
said Gran. "It will spoil the village."

"It can't be helped," said the woman. "It
has to go somewhere. I can't stop it."

Soon, big lorries and bulldozers came to
the village. Nobody wanted the motorway.
Everyone wanted to stop it, but the
bulldozers began to dig.

Gran looked at the bulldozers.
"The motorway will spoil the
countryside," she said. "Now we won't be
able to walk in the woods and go on
picnics."

The children watched the bulldozers. Biff
looked at the wild flowers.

"Oh no!" she said. "The bulldozer will
dig them up soon. Let's pick some for
Gran."

Biff and Chip made Gran a cup of tea.
They gave her the flowers.

"We picked these flowers for you," said
Chip. "The bulldozer will dig them up
soon."

Gran looked at the flowers.

"I think these flowers are very rare," she said. "I've never seen them before."
She jumped up and ran inside the house.

Gran looked in a book. She found a
picture of the flowers.

"This is wonderful!" shouted Gran.
"These flowers *are* rare. Now we can stop
the motorway."

People came from everywhere. They
looked at the rare flowers.

"This is amazing," they said. "We've
never seen these flowers before. They must
be saved."

"Hooray!" shouted Gran. "These flowers
will stop the motorway. They can't put a
motorway here. They can't dig up rare
flowers."

The rare flowers were saved, and so was Gran's village. The bulldozers and lorries went away, but they left a big hole in the ground.

"Thank you for helping us stop the
motorway," said Gran.

"What will you do about the hole?"
asked Biff.

Gran smiled. She had an idea.

The big hole was made into a lake.
Ducks came to live on it and wild flowers
grew round it.

"The children will like this," said Gran.
"It's better than a motorway."